Asian Face Reading

Unlock the Secrets
Hidden in the Human Face

Asian Face Reading

**Unlock the Secrets
Hidden in the Human Face**

Boyé Lafayette De Mente

JOURNEY EDITIONS
Boston • Rutland, Vermont • Tokyo

First published in 2003 by Journey Editions, an imprint of Periplus Editions (HK) Ltd., with editorial offices at 153 Milk Street, Boston, Massachusetts 02109.

Library of Congress Cataloging-in-Publication Data
De Mente, Boye.
Asian face reading : unlocking the secrets hidden in the human face / Boye de Mente
     p. cm.
ISBN 1-58290-067-1
     1. Physiognomy–China. 2. Physiognomy–Japan. 3. Facial expression–China. 4. Facial expression–Japan. I. Title
BF851.D37 2003
138–dc21   2003050718

Distributed by
North America, Latin America, and Europe
Tuttle Publishing
Distribution Center
Airport Industrial Park
364 Innovation Drive
North Clarendon, VT 05759-9436
Tel: (802) 773-8930
Fax: (802) 773-6993
Email: info@tuttlepublishing.com

Asia Pacific
Berkeley Books Pte. Ltd.
130 Joo Seng Road
#06-01/03 Olivine Building
Singapore 368357
Tel: (65) 6280-3320
Fax: (65) 6280-6290
Email: inquiries@periplus.com.sg

Japan
Tuttle Publishing
Yaekari Bldg., 3F
5-4-12 Ōsaki, Shinagawa-ku
Tokyo 141-0032
Tel: (03) 5437-0171
Fax: (03) 5437-0755
Email: tuttle-sales@gol.com

First edition
09 08 07 06 05 04 03   9 8 7 6 5 4 3 2 1

Design by Linda Carey
Printed in the United States of America

Contents

Preface

Face reading, a practice as old as man, is a universal art that we all use every day—with varying degrees of skill. We all know and respond to facial expressions that indicate fear, anger, merriment, and other moods, and we know from experience that facial characteristics, such as unusually large eyes or big noses, have an important influence on our lives.

But there is a great deal more to face reading than these obvious signs. The face reveals facts not only about a person's mood, but about his or her character, health, personality, sexuality, popularity, ability to make money, social status, and life expectancy as well.

And just as our faces influence our lives, life in turn changes our faces—for better or worse.

The principles of face reading, or *nin so mi* (pronounced *neen so me*), on which this book is based were first developed in China ages ago. As the generations passed in ancient China, doctors and scientists, who were members of the educated and privileged class, noted that body build and facial features had a profound influence on people's lives, from health and longevity to the degree of economic and social success they achieved. These learned men began keeping notes on their observations.

As time passed, a number of these healers and scholars wrote treatises on the relationships they discerned between the shape of the body, the head, and the facial features, and the character, personality, and other attributes of individuals. Eventually, face and body reading became a recognized profession.

The Emperor and other members of the Imperial Court as well as the elite gentry and military leaders patronized face readers in their professional as well as their private lives, further encouraging the study and use of the practice.

As Chinese learning and influence spread throughout East and Southeast Asia, the art of face reading also spread, becoming especially important in Korea and Japan, where the population was especially drawn to the practice, and it soon became an integral part of their cultures. Thereafter, the art of face reading was systematically applied in all areas of their lives, particularly in politics, business, and arranging marriages. As they did with most of the arts and crafts they imported from China, Japanese practitioners of face reading further refined and added to the scope, depth, and use of the art.

In the late 1930s, when Japan was preparing for all-out war, the Japanese air force called in a face-reading expert to study the faces of new recruits and advise on whether they should be trained as pilots, mechanics, truck drivers, and so on.

This development was what led me to take an interest in face reading. In 1954, when I was editor of *Preview* magazine in Tokyo, I learned that the face reader who had been called in by the Japanese military was still alive and lived just outside the city.

With the help of a Japanese assistant, I managed to get an interview with him and did a story about his prewar experience. This led to my doing more research on the subject at the National Diet Library, where I found a trove of treatises, old and new, on the subject.

Beginning around 1960, there was something of a face-reading renaissance in Japan, with more than a dozen scholarly works on the subject published over a period of about ten years. Face readers, along with palm readers and other soothsayers, once again became common on city sidewalks in the evenings.

In the West, on the other hand, most people regard face reading as quackery, something best associated with fortune-tellers and Gypsies.

This attitude began to change during the last decades of the twentieth century. The publication of a number of English-language books on face reading (including my own), and the appearance of professional business consultants who introduced elements of face reading into their human resources advice, resulted in the skill being taken more seriously.

By the 1990s, mainstream business publications in the United States were reporting that a growing number of leading corporations had taken to calling in face readers to help them decide on new hires as well as on promotions to managerial and executive positions.

The appearance of the Internet has been a further boon to this ancient art, with dozens of sites promoting one version or another.

Most people today would still naturally question the validity of many face-reading claims, and rightly so, because some of the interpretations are simply too esoteric—and often too contradictory—to be accepted without question.

But there are many insights that are so obvious that no one can deny them. These "readings" are so much a part of our built-in psychology and our culture that they are, in fact, accepted without question.

One of the most obvious of these readings has to do with the size, shape, and color of the eyes. An infant, male or female, with big eyes is fussed over from day one and gets special treatment. Eyes that are blue or green or streaked with gold (as are the eyes of some Vietnamese girls), get an even more dramatic reaction. The lifelong influence that big, attractive eyes have on an individual is generally profound.

The size and shape of the lips is equally powerful. Not only do they reveal a great deal about an individual's character, but they also dramatically influence the way other people behave toward that person.

Without question, the size and shape of the nose, the mouth, the teeth, and the ears tell a great deal about a person, and determine to a great extent how other people react to him or her.

The physiological and psychological foundations of face reading are as solid as physics, and knowing how to read facial and bodily features is one of the keys to developing and maintaining harmonious and effective human relationships.

As mentioned earlier, everybody reads faces, whether or not they have had any formal training. It is an automatic response. We do it without thinking. And we also react automatically in both positive and negative ways to the faces we see.

Going beyond one's naturally programmed ability to read faces can give you not only extraordinary insight into what motivates and compels people, it can also dramatically increase your ability to use the knowledge in a more positive and satisfying way.

This book covers over one hundred specific facial characteristics, some of which, admittedly, are on the unusual side. The more esoteric readings are easy to recognize and even easier to discount, but they were discovered long ago and have stood the test of time.

Curiously enough, many of the specific face readings that originated in China, Japan, and Korea are related to love and romance, no doubt because in these countries face reading played such a vital role in choosing mates for so many generations.

On the more obvious level, face reading is a skill that can be learned easily and quickly by anyone, significantly enhancing the potential for one's business and social success.

Boyé Lafayette de Mente
Tokyo, Japan

1

The ABCs of Face Reading

The Vital Power

Face reading is primarily based on the size, shape, position, quality, and color of certain facial features. Before one can read these "signs" with a maximum degree of accuracy, however, there are other factors that must be taken into consideration, the most important of which is the strength of the "vital power" of the person whose face is to be read.

Everyone is endowed with what might be called a "battery" that gives off a kind of "spark" or "light" that is reflected through the eyes, the face, and one's manner. The strength of this power varies greatly between individuals. In some people it is very feeble, and as a result they have dull eyes, dull faces, and usually lead colorless lives. In others this light may shine with startling brilliance, and such people tend to lead lives that are extraordinary in some way.

The strength of a person's "inner light" is not necessarily connected with the type of face he or she has. A person with a very "attractive" face may be low-powered, and a person whose facial features are undesirable may be a regular dynamo. And there are certain facial characteristics indicating a very low order of intelligence and imagination that are seldom accompanied by a strong life force.

Furthermore, this inner power, whatever its strength, works in different ways. One man with a powerful "battery" may become a great religious leader, while another man with the same amount of power may be a master criminal, a salesman, a writer, or a revolutionary.

A face reader can only estimate the strength of someone's vital power and its overall influence, but once he has also scrutinized the individual's facial features and body build, he can determine it more accurately.

The Body Build

Along with this inner light, the face reader must also take note of the person's body build. Most people fit into one of three broad categories: slender, stocky and muscular, or fat. And people in each of these categories share many common characteristics.

Slender men tend to be sensitive, intellectually active, emotional, have well-developed imaginative and creative powers, have love affairs with women older than themselves, and may be dominated by strong-willed women. Men of this type often do not fare well in business or politics—occupations that require physical endurance and mental toughness.

Slender women with oval-shaped faces tend to have quick minds and be skillful at manipulating men. Muscular women tend to display aggressive attitudes and behavior. They are bold and capable of playing and working hard. They tend to be less concerned about their appearance and are usually more matter-of-fact in their relations with men.

Men with muscular builds tend to prefer physical rather than mental occupations, and their answer to most problems is muscle power in one form or another. They are full of spirit, and if this spirit is not used up in work or sport, they can become frustrated and be more likely to resort to physical violence than the slender or fat man.

Muscular men usually take their sex appeal for granted, are not too demanding of women, are easier to please than the other types, and therefore are more likely to have satisfactory relations with their wives.

Both fat men and women tend to extremes of one kind or another. They are almost always friendly and jovial, but they can also be unusually cruel. And they have a tendency to indulge themselves in physical pleasures.

The Facial Alignment

One of the most important signs in face reading is whether the right and left sides of the face are balanced. The more unbalanced a person's face, the more likely he or she will be psychologically troubled and suffer hardships and disappointments in life.

Just as the brain is divided into two sections with different functions, the sides of the face reflect different things. Usually one side of the face is "positive" and one side is "negative." One side reveals "conscious" aspects of personality, the other side "unconscious" issues.

In most people, the left side of the face indicates character and temperament, while the right side portrays emotions, social and economic position, and interpersonal relations with others.

According to face-reading theory, the front of the face reveals the "public" side of a person, while the sides are more expressive of the "private" side.

The Three Types of Faces

There are three basic types of faces, each of which corresponds to a specific kind of character and fortune. These three types are triangular, round, and square.

The Triangular Face

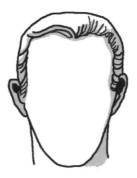

A person with a triangular face tends to be an intellectual and a dreamer, and may run from one extreme to another. Men with triangular faces are often shy and self-conscious. Most great philosophers, musicians, and writers fall into this category.

Some of the features that are common to men with triangular faces are a high but narrow forehead, thin-pointed chin, dark skin, long thin nose, large thin ears, facial unbalance from left to right, and a shifty expression.

If the features of the triangular face are exceptionally unbalanced and abnormal, the individual is more likely to have a cruel nature or suffer from insanity.

The Square Face

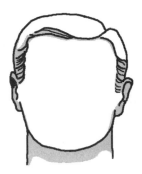

Individuals with square or "athletic" faces usually have a wide, low forehead with a straight chin, thick lips, thick nose, large ears, and good overall facial balance. This type of face is most often found in men and is indicative of strong will, self-confidence, a practical nature, and the ability to influence others. Many well-known political leaders have square faces (and square heads).

The Round Face

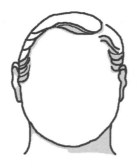

The round-faced person usually has a fleshy face with large, full cheeks, a large mouth, narrow forehead, thick lips, a short, thick nose, and thick ears. The overall facial balance is typically uneven.

Round-faced men are usually very adaptable, aggressive, methodical, and practical. They generally like sophisticated food and fashionable clothing, and are apt to consider themselves playboys. Women with round faces are usually gregarious and sociable, preferring to be with others at all times. They are also apt to be wildly enthusiastic about one thing after another.

The Three Zones of Fortune

Asian fortune-tellers, who base most of their predictions on nin so mi, divide the face horizontally into three zones: the forehead, the area from the eyebrows to the bottom of the nose, and from the bottom of the nose to the chin.

The forehead is said to be the most revealing during one's youth, the middle "zone" during middle age, and the bottom area during old age. The forehead, also referred to as the "upper zone," is said to indicate one's parental heritage and is the area most subject to change during youth.

The middle zone, which includes the eyebrows, nose, eyes, and cheeks, is most important during a person's middle years, reflecting not only the past and present, but the future as well.

The lower zone—the mouth and chin—indicates what kind of fortune a person will have after he or she passes the age of forty, and is exceptionally revealing about one's emotions, morality, compassion, and sexual attitudes.

2

What the Forehead Foretells

High and Wide Foreheads

Most people regard a high and wide forehead as a sign of intelligence and energy. Face readers agree. They say this type of forehead also indicates a person who spends a lot of time observing and meditating. When an individual's forehead is high, wide, richly fleshed, and unblemished, other people tend to treat that person in a positive, helpful way, giving him or her more opportunities and therefore a better chance in life. The high, wide forehead is therefore very common among successful people—especially men.

Low and Wide Foreheads

This type of forehead is a sign both of unusual intelligence and keen powers of observation. Although generally not as indicative of intelligence as the high and wide forehead, the low and wide forehead indicates patience and perseverance—qualities that contribute a great deal to the success of people in this category.

One characteristic of people with low and wide foreheads is that they are often so self-conscious they are unable to realize their full potential.

High and Narrow Foreheads

A person with a high and narrow forehead is regarded by face readers as tending to be hard-hearted and indifferent to others, although very intelligent. Many scientists have this type of forehead. Other facial features that are positive may offset some of the negative influences of the high, narrow forehead.

Low and Narrow Foreheads

Face readers agree with the commonly held belief that a low, narrow forehead is generally a sign indicating irresponsibility, carelessness, dishonesty, and, in many cases, brutality. Men with this type of forehead may be smart and clever, but they are seldom really intelligent. About the only legitimate profession in which such men reach high positions is politics.

Unbalanced Foreheads

The unbalanced forehead, on which the hair grows farther down on one side than on the other, is regarded by face readers as an indication of intellectual disharmony and emotional discontent.

In young boys and girls this type of forehead may indicate a tendency toward delinquency. According to face-reading theory, women with this type of forehead tend to be opportunistic and unscrupulous.

The negative response of others explains at least in part the behavior of people with this feature. The factor can be partly if not completely eliminated by styling the hair a certain way or by shaving the low side of the hairline to create a balance.

Blemished Foreheads

A conspicuously visible scar or any other blemish on the forehead is said to have an unusually adverse affect on a person's fortune, and the closer the scar is to the center of the forehead the more serious the consequences are apt to be.

Such blemishes are regarded as especially serious because the area of the forehead between the eyes is the focal point of the body—"the center of the life force." Any fault in this area will have a strongly unfavorable influence on everyone with whom the person comes in contact, and as a result affects the person's life in many ways.

A mole anywhere on a person's forehead will also adversely affect his or her life. If a woman has a forehead mole, face-reading theory predicts that she is likely to have an unhappy marriage.

But a mole on an eyebrow is regarded as a sign of good luck, especially where money is concerned. Furthermore, a mole between the eyes or on one of the cheeks may be considered a beauty mark.

A mole between the eyes gives an impression of gravity and calm. One on the cheek breaks up the balance of the face, but if it is positioned harmoniously it gives the impression that the person is friendly, playful, and consequently charming.

A mole or beauty spot on the right side of the face has a

stronger influence than one on the left because most people when talking with another person focus their attention on the right side of that person's face. The closer a beauty spot is to the eyes, the greater the influence—because the eyes are the center of one's expression.

A woman with a beauty spot near her eyes will frequently have a matching spot on her chest—or so says face-reading lore. Lore also says that if a beauty spot is located near her lips the matching spot will be lower on her body.

Complexion of the Forehead

The complexion of a person's forehead reveals his or her personality like a neon sign. When one is going through a bad time, the forehead tends to take on a dark, unhealthy appearance.

When the forehead is clear and its color is vivid, a person is much less likely to have any kind of difficulty. If a person's forehead is discolored and clears up, his or her fortune will also improve.

Any type of worry or bad luck causes the forehead to lose its vividness, but it is especially sensitive to marriage problems and a failure to gain desired public recognition.

Forehead Wrinkles

There are several common patterns of forehead wrinkles that face readers can interpret at a glance. These include: (a) one long horizontal wrinkle; (b) two long horizontal wrinkles; (c) three or more long horizontal wrinkles; (d) three long horizontal wrinkles with the middle one "broken" in a number of places; (e) many short, thin wrinkles all over the forehead; (f) several deep, curved wrinkles covering the center of the forehead; (g) several short wave-shaped wrinkles; (h) a few wrinkles that are "geese" shaped, along with one, two, or three deep, vertical wrinkles between the eyebrows.

One Forehead Wrinkle

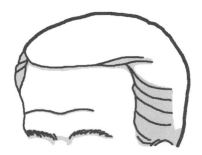

People with narrow foreheads are most apt to have one long horizontal wrinkle, which is usually well below the centerline. This type of wrinkle and forehead is an indication that the person had a rough time when young.

One forehead wrinkle is generally a sign of lower than average intelligence and an opportunistic and greedy nature. Individuals with this facial feature may, however, be especially hard workers and succeed in business and other pursuits despite their handicap.

As in all negative facial features, the overall effect results from a double whammy—from the inherent character of the individual and from the reaction of other people to the person with the feature.

Two Forehead Wrinkles

Two long forehead wrinkles are said to be indicative of two important areas of life: one's personal relations with others and one's popularity and health. If the top wrinkle is shorter and thinner than the bottom line it is a sign that the individual may not be able to depend upon friends and associates (because they will not value the relationship that highly).

If the top line is full and pronounced and the second line is long and deep, it is a sign that the individual is especially popular among friends and people in general and would have an advantage in politics.

Three Forehead Wrinkles

Three parallel wrinkles on the forehead are a sign of quick perception and good memory. The deeper the lines the more a person has worried and the harder he or she has worked.

If other facial features are favorable, people with three forehead wrinkles have a very good chance for success in life.

Many Thin Wrinkles

Thin wrinkles all over the forehead in no particular pattern are a sign of mental fatigue or a breakdown in health. Women with this type of forehead are said to suffer from physical defects that prevent them from enjoying life fully. Men with this forehead often have diverse interests and divide their time and energy to the point that they may not succeed in any of them.

Many Convex Wrinkles

Several deep, roughly convex wrinkles in the center of the forehead are a sign of low intelligence and general ineptitude—and men are more likely to have this feature than women.

Women are not attracted to men with this feature, and there is a tendency for these men to marry late. They generally do not know how to express affection, and are likely to be unsophisticated and dull. This does not mean, however, that they cannot be successful on a relatively low level, because they may be very hardworking, diligent, and loyal to friends and employers.

It goes without saying that when women have this forehead feature, it is a turn-off to men. Fortunately, this feature does not develop until middle age, and prior to the onset of middle age, women with this characteristic may have other physical attributes that men find attractive.

Wavy-Line Wrinkles

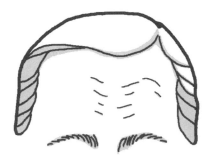

People with irregularly patterned, wavy-line forehead wrinkles are said to generally be from "good" families but to have had sad experiences during childhood. These people are rarely ambitious or talented enough to become successful in early life, and tend to bumble along until they are well past middle age, at which time they may settle down and enjoy some measure of success.

Women with this type of forehead are said to be fated to suffer ill health and problems with their husbands.

"Wild Geese" Wrinkles

According to face-reading theory, "wild geese" wrinkles (wrinkles that look like a front view of geese in flight) are indicative of a person who is not very courageous and whose talents tend to be narrow.

Men who have "wild geese" wrinkles are generally not very concerned about money or the everyday problems of life, and do not make good husbands. They like to work alone and do not care for socializing. Geniuses frequently have foreheads of this type.

Faint Wrinkles or No Wrinkles

People without conspicuous forehead wrinkles of any kind, or with wrinkles that are light and mostly on the right side, are seldom successful in any endeavor until their late thirties or early forties. Then their abilities, whatever they may be, develop rapidly and they go on to reach their maximum potential. Men and women who have "baby faces" tend to be in this category (no wrinkles or very faint ones)—if for no other reason than people do not take them seriously before they reach middle age.

An obvious plus is that such people continue to look young when in their senior years, to their great advantage in both business and personal relationships.

One Wrinkle Between the Eyebrows

One vertical wrinkle between the eyebrows is a conspicuous sign of strong will and equally strong stubbornness. People with this feature refuse to give up or give in once they start something, and whatever success they achieve is apt to be a result of their perseverance rather than their intelligence or talents.

People with one vertical wrinkle between their eyebrows are generally not very passionate, and their relationships with husbands and wives tend to be platonic and perfunctory. This latter characteristic may be somewhat mitigated by larger than usual eyes, but more likely than not, the person with this feature will have small eyes.

Two Wrinkles Between the Eyebrows

Two wrinkles between the eyebrows are said to indicate strong critical powers and a highly developed sense of justice. Men with this characteristic tend to be kind and considerate toward others, and to have affectionate relationships with their spouses and other members of the opposite sex.

Where women are concerned, however, two creases between the eyebrows may mean trouble. Their strong sense of justice and sexual equality may lead them to be overly possessive about their husbands' attentions, and result in jealousy.

Generally, people who have this feature are also blessed with other positive facial features, such as good balance, large eyes, attractive eyebrows, and so on.

Oblique Wrinkles Between the Eyebrows

Either oblique or horizontal wrinkles between the eyebrows are regarded as a sign of a bad temper and a tendency to do foolish things while having tantrums. Generally speaking, people with this forehead feature fail to mature properly and continue to exhibit behavior that is more typical of young children.

It is often possible to predict which children—both boys and girls—are going to develop this particular facial feature from their behavior while young. This is one situation in which it is possible to help people avoid developing a decidedly negative facial feature by influencing their behavior and personality while they are young.

The Fortune Key

A vertical strip on the forehead, about an inch wide and extending from the hairline down to the line of the eyebrows, is said to have considerable influence on one's acceptance by others, and therefore has a great deal to do with determining a person's social and financial success.

If this area is clear of faults and is attractive in both color and form, it usually indicates an abundance of spiritual and physical energy, and is a sign that the person will be treated well and therefore have a better chance of developing his or her full potential.

By the same token, the more unattractive this "fortune key," the more serious the handicap—not so much from the inherent deficiencies of the individual concerned but because of the way people react to him or her.

The Forehead Horns

If the two bony areas above a person's eyes protrude like horns, this is taken to indicate that he or she had a rough time during childhood, and the feature remains a serious handicap throughout life. Men with these horns tend to be overly aggressive, while women tend to be flighty and reckless. Obviously, this feature is genetically determined, which means that these individuals start out with a physical handicap that often becomes more pronounced as they grow older and are influenced (molded) by their own behavior as well as by the reaction of others.

The Money Luck Sign

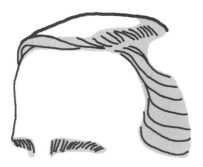

An area just above the inner edge of the eyebrow and near the nose is said to indicate one's moneymaking ability. If the bony structure of this area is conspicuously high, it is said that the individual is likely to be poor at making money and will not fare well in either business or politics.

People with scars or faults in this area are likely to be plagued by money problems, and in the event that they do succeed in achieving a significant degree of success, there is a good chance they will lose whatever money they have made or suffer some other disaster.

If this area should become discolored or the skin becomes withered, it is regarded as a sign that bad luck in money matters will follow. On the other hand, if this area is conspicuously smooth and clear, it will not only bring luck to people in making money, but it is also a sign that they will be able to enjoy their good fortune.

Again, the influence of this facial feature is based more on the reaction of other people to the individual than on the ability and ambitions of the person concerned. The point being that it is not so much who and what we are but how other people perceive us, and react to us, that affects our lives for good or bad.

The Friendship Spot

In face-reading theory, the area just above the eyebrows is directly linked to how one gets along with friends, or so-called friends. Any kind of suppressed friction between friends is said to result in this area becoming dark reddish in color, which is an indication that the relationship is going to deteriorate and bring suffering.

The darker this area becomes the more serious the problem, and the more likely the person will suffer serious harm from someone regarded as a friend. If the area is reddish but not dark, however, face readers say the problem with a friend more likely concerns a competitive situation involving a job or a relationship with someone else.

The "Vitality" Spot

The area between the eyebrows, directly above any wrinkles, is considered one of the most important keys to predicting a person's fortune, particularly in matters of life and death. This spot, according to nin so mi experts, indicates one's "life vitality."

If the flesh in this area is raised and clear, it is taken as a sign of great vitality, and indicates that the individual—although usually independent and a loner—is responsible and a hard worker, with an excellent chance of playing an important role in society.

It is also considered a favorable sign if this area is flat but mirror like in appearance. Men with this characteristic are regarded as lucky and able to recover from almost any disaster. Their potential is said to be virtually unlimited. They get along exceptionally well with people and typically get extraordinary help and support from friends and associates.

In women, this sign is said to indicate unusual intelligence and a friendly personality, which in turn contributes to their being popular and successful in relationships with men. Any flaws in this important area are regarded as an especially serious handicap and are likely to spoil a person's chance for success in any field where he or she must have the active cooperation of others. Face-reading principles say that people tend to resent the opinions or leadership of those who have a flawed "vital spot."

Men with a flaw in this area are advised to take up occupations in which they can work independently. Women with flaws in the same area are usually not very popular, and generally do not have the advantage of the support and close friendship of others. They are advised not to be very critical or expect too much in their relationships with men.

A mole on the "vitality spot" is one of the worst kinds of flaws. Women with vitality-spot moles are said to be difficult to get along with, and unless the moles are removed the flaw leads to one piece of back luck after another.

Any change in the color or texture of the skin in this area is also regarded as an unmistakable forewarning of trouble. Any darkening of the area is especially bad, and the darker it becomes the greater the misfortune that is likely to occur. If the skin becomes coarse it is very likely a symptom of a serious illness.

The Artist's Forehead

Men and women whose foreheads and hairlines combine to form the shape of an *M* usually have highly developed creative powers, and often become painters, writers, editors, musicians, or actors. People with the *M* forehead are also usually very successful in such occupations as planning and designing, but they tend to be emotional and often have difficulty working for people who live by the numbers.

The *M* feature signals sensitivity to the needs of others.

The Practical Person's Forehead

This type of forehead is more common in—and more characteristic of—men. Men with square foreheads are seldom successful in early life, but are noted for being practical, scrupulous, and willing to work for long years to accomplish goals. Most tend to be businessmen or go into some branch of science where such attributes are advantageous.

Women with square foreheads tend to be more ambitious and aggressive in their attitudes, with the result that they frequently clash with others.

Women with square foreheads that are disfigured by scars or other faults are regarded as especially unlucky because this tends to contribute to marriage problems and divorce. Those with square foreheads can mitigate some of its influence through hair styling and makeup.

The Rounded Forehead

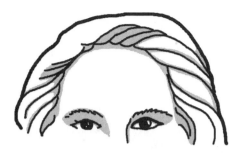

Women with rounded foreheads are believed by face readers to be destined to become divorcées or widows because they tend to marry men who are worthless or in poor health. Fortune-tellers advise women in this category to acquire a profession so that they will be able to support themselves. They are also advised that their chances of making a better marriage a second time are very slim.

Men with round foreheads, on the other hand, are considered lucky because they tend to be good-natured and easy to get along with—although they generally are not aggressive enough to achieve outstanding success in highly competitive professions.

The Female Forehead

Just as the square forehead is associated with men, a crescent-shaped forehead—so-called because the hairline and forehead form twin crescents—is most often found in women.

Women with this type of forehead hairline are usually home- and family-oriented, and are very affectionate. They are also very susceptible to the attentions of men, fall in love easily, and often suffer as a result.

Men with crescent-shaped foreheads tend to be somewhat less aggressive in their attitudes and behavior. They are usually most attracted to women with strong, aggressive personalities.

Protruding Foreheads

Some people have convex-like foreheads that protrude or jut out, and regardless of whether or not their foreheads are also high and wide, this is generally a sure sign of independence, adaptability, resourcefulness, and brilliance.

Both men and women with convex foreheads usually do well in business, particularly in businesses that require them to be popular with the public or their customers. These people mix well and are quick to take advantage of their surroundings.

This type of forehead, however, does not contribute to an ideal home- or family-oriented marriage, particularly if both husband and wife have protruding foreheads. But if just the husband, or just the wife, has a jutting forehead it usually means he or she will spend most of the time away from home, deeply involved in some kind of enterprise, and the marriage can be harmonious.

Sunken Foreheads

Some people have foreheads that are concave—a physical trait that is extraordinarily conspicuous and has an equally extraordinary effect on their lives. There is a tendency for people with sunken foreheads to be automatically regarded as below par in intelligence and other desirable characteristics. But that is not necessarily so.

Writers, painters, and politicians often fall into this category; however, their foreheads are usually distinguished by a number of long parallel wrinkles—a sign of concentration and steadfastness to their ideals and goals. They tend to have very narrow interests.

If the forehead of a person in this category is lined with many wrinkles without any pattern, he or she tends to be a very hard worker and to be good at making money; yet such people are regarded by face readers as unreliable.

A concave forehead in conjunction with a proportionately long nose and a small, receding chin is especially bad news. People with these facial features are generally less intelligent than the average, have less vitality, and are usually physically weaker than most others.

Because of these handicaps, and because people tend to treat them as inferior, such people often become dropouts from the mainstream of life.

High Eyebrow Bones

Generally speaking, the more a person's eyebrow bones protrude, the more aggressive he or she tends to be—the feature is characteristically a male trait. People with low eyebrow bones tend to be passive and weak in both physical energy and spirit, whether male or female.

Men with high eyebrow bones are usually vigorous and active, and believe in the application of power to overcome obstacles or enemies, while those with low eyebrow bones are more apt to take the path of least resistance.

Low eyebrow bones are mostly found in women. Women who have noticeably high eyebrow bones also tend to be noticeably more aggressive in their attitudes and behavior.

Neanderthal men and women, along with our contemporary primate cousins, were noted for their high eyebrow bones, indicating that some present-day *Homo sapiens* are not that far removed from their ancestors.

3

What the Eyebrows Reveal

Signs of Longevity

Eyebrow hair is directly associated with health, longevity, and romance. People with very thin eyebrow hair tend to be especially susceptible to illnesses and to have limited life spans. It is said that the appearance of one or more gray hairs in the eyebrows during youth is a warning of bad health to come.

Thick eyebrows are associated with strength, courage, and other positive attributes. Women with conspicuously thick eyebrows are believed to be capable of bearing many children.

Long hair in the eyebrows, particularly when it is coupled with long hair in the ears, is regarded as one of the most dependable signs of longevity. The longer and bushier the eyebrow hair, the more powerful the individual's life force tends to be. Men and women who live beyond the age of eighty are almost always distinguished by heavy dark eyebrows, since eyebrows are the last body hairs to turn gray.

"Unloving Wife" Eyebrows

In face-reading theory, women with exceptionally long and beautiful eyebrows are poor choices for wives because they characteristically cannot develop frank, affectionate relationships with their husbands.

The reasons for this trait, according to nin so mi, is that when young, these women were loved and pampered to excess by their parents and relatives, making it difficult or impossible for them to develop satisfying relationships later in life with their husbands. Many women who do not naturally have long beautiful eyebrows, and were not spoiled when young, use makeup to lengthen and beautify their eyebrows, thereby reaping some of the benefits.

"Poverty" Eyebrows

In the face-reader's handbook, eyebrows that are conspicuously short are a bad sign. Short eyebrows are closely associated with poverty and a lack of affection during childhood and youth.

People in this category are considered especially unlucky because they usually cannot depend on getting any kind of help from family or friends in any of their endeavors.

Ancient Chinese texts on face reading indicate that men with short eyebrows typically attempt to make up for the affection they missed during childhood by being romantically adventurous in later life.

If such men are unsuccessful in their relationships with women, the face-reading texts add, they will typically turn to violence and criminal activity.

People with short eyebrows that are thick enough to be called "bushy" are inclined to be obstinate and to have terrible tempers.

"Late Bloomer" Eyebrows

Eyebrow hair that is thick and grows close to the eyes is regarded as a sign that the person is not resourceful or flexible, and will have trouble establishing himself or herself until late in life.

Asian fortune-tellers advise "late bloomers" with this type of eyebrow that it is better for them not to marry until they are in their late twenties or early thirties because they are not likely to achieve financial stability until they are middle-aged or older.

When a person with "late bloomer" eyebrows has an *M*-shaped forehead hairline—that is, the hairline forms the shape of an *M*—it is indicative of a distinctive artistic ability of very high order.

"Seducer" Eyebrows

Nin so mi says that people with very thin eyebrows have not had a happy family life and, particularly, received little or no affection from their parents.

Men with this type of eyebrow are said to be clever and resourceful, especially at manipulating women. But they are also said to be cowardly, and are often involved in conflicts because of their attraction to women.

Women with especially thin eyebrows are often taken advantage of by men because they lack confidence and the courage to be aggressive and defend themselves. Many women with this feature, reacting subconsciously, thicken and expand their eyebrows with makeup.

Pleasure Seeker Eyebrows

Crescent-shaped eyebrows that are beautiful in both form and quality are regarded as feminine and are said to indicate especially strong emotional values and needs. Women with conspicuously crescent-shaped eyebrows are said to be pleasure-seekers, to be artistic and good-natured, and to be loved by everybody. But after a period of social success, such women often fall prey to men who will take advantage of them.

Men with long, crescent-shaped eyebrows are usually not aggressive and depend more on the patronage of friends and superiors—especially on their women friends—than on their own talents or efforts. Such men are also said to be especially sensitive. Both men and women with crescent-shaped eyebrows more often than not are from well-to-do families.

There are numerous examples of women in the entertainment industries, particularly movie and TV stars, who either have naturally crescent-shaped eyebrows or create them with makeup.

Masculine Eyebrows

A thick eyebrow that forms a straight or almost straight line is known as a "masculine" eyebrow. Men who have this kind of eyebrow tend to be overtly ambitious, aggressive, straightforward, and to persevere in their efforts to achieve their goals.

Men with conspicuously masculine eyebrows tend to keep their emotions under control to the point that they are often oblivious to the feelings of others. They are apt to go through life without giving or receiving more than a token measure of affection.

Women who have purely masculine eyebrows tend to be just as ambitious and aggressive in their attitudes and behavior. They are usually less attractive to men than women with other kinds of eyebrows, display less affection than is typical of other women, and can appear cold.

As a result of their nature, women in this group often have unhappy marriages, particularly when they marry men with similar personality traits.

Those women who pluck their eyebrows so they are in a straight line are generally not aware of the message they are sending to both men and other women.

Amazon Eyebrows

Women whose eyebrows are shaped like a twig bent at an abrupt angle near one end are said to have unusually strong romantic inclinations and to be very demanding of their male friends and partners.

Such women typically are not satisfied with one man and may remain single in order to have many male friends. When they do marry they are likely to exercise great power over their husbands.

Amazon eyebrows are also regarded as a sure sign that a woman will have luck with money.

Bent-twig eyebrows on men are also regarded as positive because it indicates they have a strong spirit and are aggressive and proud, but these traits are tempered by an affectionate nature.

Many women around the world, responding to an unconscious impulse, make up their eyebrows in the bent-twig shape even though it is not natural for them.

Male makeup artists catering to actresses and models invariably give them crescent or bent-twig eyebrows because they subconsciously know those shapes are the most appealing to men.

Eyebrows Close Together

Some people have eyebrows that have very little distance between them. In some extreme cases their eyebrows join above the nose, resulting in one long line of brow hair instead of two.

This kind of eyebrow sends out negative signals for both men and women. Where men are concerned, the negative influence of eyebrows that are joined or nearly joined is often strong enough to prevent them from achieving success if their chosen field depends on the good will and receptive behavior of others.

Some men with this kind of eyebrow who are also exceptionally talented and persistent are able to overcome its negative influence and achieve success after they pass the age of forty.

Obviously, men who are aware of the negative influence of joined eyebrows can remedy the situation simply by plucking or shaving the hair bridging the nose.

Even if the eyebrows are of a light color, if they meet across the nose, face readers regard them as negative and counsel removing them. The few women who have joined eyebrows are generally wise enough to pluck them without any outside counseling.

Extravagant Eyebrows

Not surprisingly, eyebrows that are conspicuously far apart—but not to an extreme—have positive readings, just as those that are joined, or are "too close together," are negative.

Wide-apart eyebrows give an open, expansive, intelligent impression, and people who have them are treated better than people who don't have them. People with extravagant eyebrows also feel much better about themselves and are more confident in their abilities and the things they do.

The advantage of wide-apart eyebrows comes early, and often contributes to both men and women achieving success before they reach the age of thirty.

There is such a thing as the eyes and the eyebrows being too far apart, however, and when this occurs it is decidedly negative because it comes across as a deformity.

Men with eyebrows that are unusually but not excessively far apart are categorized as being overly extravagant in their behavior, which sometimes has a correspondingly negative effect on their lives.

Vertical Eyebrows

People notice the eyebrows first when they look at each other, and if there is anything at all different about them it has both a conscious and subconscious impact on how we view and treat the other person.

Among the most conspicuous of all eyebrows are so-called vertical eyebrows. In such eyebrows the hair grows more or less upward rather than horizontal, not only giving people a peculiar look but also sending a loud signal about their character.

For some unknown reason, people with this eyebrow trait are noted for being especially tenacious and persistent in whatever they set out to do. They never give up no matter how many or what kind of obstacles they encounter—and there is no satisfactory explanation as to which came first, the upswept eyebrows or the tenacious behavior.

Weeping Eyebrows

When people cry they tend to scrunch up their eyebrows, making them unpleasant to look at. Some people have eyebrows that always look like they are crying. The message sent by "weeping eyebrows" is that the person is unfriendly and a chronic complainer. People with such eyebrows tend to always look at the dark side of things and to always be depressed.

People who have weeping eyebrows generally accomplish very little before marriage, and after marriage they generally make life miserable for their spouses and children. Their negativism is often strong enough that it not only ruins their lives, it also prevents their spouses from achieving their potential in business.

It should be noted, however, that there are occasional exceptions to this rule. Some people whose first marriages fail are able to suppress the influences that affect people in this category when they marry a second time, especially if their new partners are easy to get along with and earn good money.

4

Reading the Eyes

The "Glitter" of the Eyes

The size, shape, and condition of the eyes reveal many things about a person's character, personality, inclinations, abilities, and fortune. But all of these are secondary to the "glitter" or inner power that appears in the eyes. The amount of inner power that shines in a person's eyes varies with the individual. In some people it glows brilliantly; in others it is only a faint ember.

Eyes that sparkle with spirit, energy, and vivaciousness will overcome many weaknesses in a person's face, and the best face is instantly betrayed if the eyes do not have a certain amount of this divine spark.

Glitter alone is not enough to make "ideal" eyes, because when glitter appears by itself it is a sign that the person's spirit—from which the glitter comes—is uncontrolled and may therefore be dangerous. The eyes of those who are very cruel, fanatical, or insane often shine with such intensity they appear nonhuman.

The most desirable eyes are those that shine brilliantly and also have in them a quality that is called "spirit of peace," which flows from one's inherent kindness, friendliness, and compassion.

Both this glitter and spirit of peace may appear in eyes of any shape or size, and whether or not these qualities are present and in what strength is of primary importance in reading a person's character and fortune.

Balance of the Eyes

There is one other vital point the face reader must make note of before looking at the physical features of the eyes, and that is their balance in the face. The more nearly perfectly the elements of the face are balanced horizontally and vertically the better. An imbalance of the features relays a negative message—not to mention the fact that the individual with an unbalanced forehead, or eyes or mouth, is also negatively influenced by the defect, even when he or she is not consciously aware of the fault.

Of course, the more pronounced the imbalance of the eyes the more adverse the effect on the person's fortune.

Fortunately, few people's eyes are perfectly balanced, so there is some tolerance for what is acceptable without any penalty. Furthermore, a moderate degree of imbalance does not mean that the individual is mentally defective in any way, and most people are able to easily compensate for the disadvantage.

Many people overcome this particular handicap with humor, as is evidenced by a number of well-known professional entertainers (both male and female) who are far from handsome and use their uneven faces to their advantage.

Male and Female Eyes

It sometimes happens that a person's eyes are different in both size and shape. When this difference is quite conspicuous, face readers refer to such eyes as being "male and female."

Men with one eye larger than the other are said to be fortunate. They are described in face-reading lore as being especially ambitious and resourceful. They are typically outgoing, aggressive, and are more successful than usual at making money.

Women with one "male" and one "female" eye commonly have had both good and bad experiences in life. They generally really like men, know instinctively how to please them, and are therefore popular with the opposite sex.

But women with "unisex" eyes are unusually susceptible to the amorous approaches of men, and have difficulty saying no to them. Because of this they are apt to experience marital problems. They learn from experience, however, and are usually more successful during a second marriage.

In some people the male and female eye feature is so conspicuous that they become acutely aware of it just from seeing their faces in mirrors, and they suffer from knowing that they have an imbalance. Women can counter some of the negative effects of unbalanced eyes with makeup.

If their eyes are unbalanced enough to elicit comments from others, they can mitigate much of the undesirable effect by humorous remarks.

The Large-Eye Bonus

The old adage "Your face is your fortune" is never more true than when it comes to the size of your eyes, particularly if you have large eyes. Large eyes come in two sizes: large and over-whelming. Men with eyes that are so large they are very conspic-uous are generally very emotional, artistic, and full of fighting spirit. They are apt to be radical in both thought and action, and to become involved in revolutionary projects.

Men with huge eyes are usually very attractive to women. On the negative side, such men tend to be moody and lack persever-ance. If they do not succeed at something quickly they are likely to give it up and start something else.

Males with eyes that are large but not overwhelming start out life with a big advantage. During their childhood and youth they are favored by almost everyone with whom they come into con-tact, and they continue to have this advantage throughout life.

A baby girl born with large eyes is considered something spe-cial and is fussed over and admired by everyone. This special treatment continues, and by the time the girl is in her teens both men and women are irresistibly drawn to her.

If the large-eyed girl is ambitious and clever she can use oth-ers to reach her goals. She has a much better chance of making a good marriage and being a success socially and financially than girls with smaller eyes.

Girls and women with large eyes tend to be sensitive and, if they have sufficient "glitter" in their eyes, artistic. They do especially well in the entertainment trades whether or not their talent is of a very high caliber.

Women with exceptionally large eyes, however, often have serious problems, because they are used to being catered to and don't know how to develop a close, mutually satisfying relationship with a man. The typically spirited independence of women who have large eyes can be upsetting to the men who marry them. As a result, the likelihood of them divorcing and remarrying one or more times is stronger than usual.

If teenage girls or women have exceptionally large eyes that lack "power," they will attract men the way blossoms attract honeybees, but they will not be able to control them—or how they react to them.

Small Eyes

People with small eyes seldom enjoy conspicuous success during their younger years. However, they tend to be practical pluggers, strong-willed, and steadfast. If small-eyed people are able to get a good education, their chance for success in business or politics is good. But without an education, they are more likely to become field or factory workers.

A conspicuous amount of inner power in small eyes is a sign that the individual is not "ordinary," and that he or she cannot be expected to always conform. Such people are especially prone to having serious financial difficulties.

People with small eyes are less likely to be artistically inclined than their big-eyed counterparts, and when they are in the entertainment industry it is usually because of some skill or attribute that is not necessarily related to their appearance—as with character actors and comedians.

And, of course, the smaller a person's eyes, the more negative the message they send to the outside world, and the more difficult it is for them to overcome the small-eye prejudice that seems to be inherent in *Homo sapiens*.

Goggle Eyes

So-called goggle eyes come in two types. In one type the upper eyelid is thin and the eyeballs protrude noticeably. In the other, the bulge of the eyeballs is less pronounced, and the upper eyelid is thick or puffy.

People in the first category are good at mind-reading and tend to be cautious, passive, and timid. They are usually quite intelligent and very susceptible to the opposite sex.

Men with goggle eyes and thin upper eyelids tend to be overconfident in their ability to "handle" women, and as a result often have problems with their female friends—and wives.

Women with the same kind of eyes and upper eyelids, on the other hand, are usually very skillful at maintaining harmonious relations with men, and generally have happy marriages. But they tend to be plagued by problems with their children.

Men with the second type of goggle eyes—less protruding eyeballs and thick upper eyelids—tend to be extraordinarily energetic, courageous, and ambitious.

They prefer their own business to working for other people, and since they do practically nothing but work they are very apt to be financially successful sooner or later, no matter how many obstacles they have to overcome.

Women in this category share many of the characteristics of the men, particularly in being energetic, capable, and ambitious. Men are sensually attracted to them, but their personality tends to clash with that of men.

One of the results of this clash between goggled-eyed women with thick upper eyelids and men in the same category is that the women often marry men who are less desirable as husbands. However, such women are generally very good in business, especially in handling large numbers of employees.

The Hollow-Eyes Syndrome

 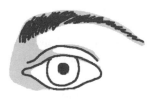

Some people are born with what face-reading lore refers to as "hollow eyes," or "metal-pot eyes." They are a clear sign of a lack of confidence, mental clumsiness, poor speech, and the inability to express affection or love.

People with such eyes generally succeed only when caution and tenacity pay off. Any success they attain usually comes late in life and is the fruit of years of steady toiling.

Women with hollow eyes are not very interested in men and make little or no effort to appear attractive. They basically do not know how to react to men and, with occasional exceptions, are generally insensitive to both beauty and ugliness.

When such women marry it is often at a later age than usual, and is usually to men who are significantly older than they are or are less desirable as spouses for other reasons. It is said that women with hollow eyes will have smooth marriages if their husbands are easygoing and not much interested in socializing.

Interestingly, some hollow-eyed women have a creative impulse that leads them to take up writing or painting—another example of how the human spirit can and often does overcome the challenges people face.

Eyes Close Together

The "normal" distance between the eyes is said to be the horizontal length of one eye. Men with eyes that are closer than this standard are considered to be adaptable but flighty, and to have a tendency to change occupations frequently. Women with close-set eyes are said to be good talkers and clever at telling what others are thinking but inordinately jealous and prone to irrational behavior when things don't go their way.

In nature's way, eyes that are closer together than they should be are also generally smaller than the optimum size for the face they adorn—adding to their overall influence on both the individual and others. Fortunately, many people with this problem are able to overcome all or most of its negative influence through their spirit and by developing compensating characteristics.

Eyes Far Apart

Eyes that are conspicuously farther apart than normal are read as a sign of impatience, mental dullness, and a lack of drive. People with this feature seldom have strong opinions and therefore make good followers. They are very susceptible to being led into trouble if they associate with unscrupulous people, and should not be given work that requires mental alertness or speed. They are best suited for activity that is simple and repetitive.

Shifty Eyes

So-called shifty eyes are said to be indicative of strong emotions and are usually a sign that the person is sensitive to what others are thinking. When a person constantly shifts his or her eyes from left to right it is regarded as a sign of mental turmoil, caution, and insincerity. Looking upward frequently when someone else is talking is a well-known sign of boredom or disapproval. Looking downward is a sign of shyness or a guilty conscience, and is so common that everyone recognizes its meaning.

Shifting the eyes from left to right while looking downward is a sign of cowardice and selfishness and is characteristic of a person who will inform on others to save himself or herself. Excessive blinking is a sign of nervousness and mental fatigue.

Secret Lover Eyes

Face readers say that a droplet of moisture between the eyeball and the lower eyelid is a sign that the person is involved in a passionate love affair. If a married woman has this fresh "dewdrop" in her eyes it is said to be a sign that she has a secret lover.

This "dewdrop" should not be confused with tears or the eyes watering from some irritation—making it difficult if not impossible to read this signal correctly.

Large Pupils

In addition to variations in overall eye size, the pupils also range from small to large and have a great deal to do with character. Not surprisingly, the larger the pupils the more positive the reading. Large pupils, according to nin so mi experts, are almost always a sure sign that the individual has a peaceful disposition and is gentle and kind.

Men with large eye pupils are said to make the best husbands, best friends, and the best business associates because they are the most likely to sublimate their own desires on behalf of others. The same characteristics apply to women with large eye pupils, with the result that an ideal couple is one in which both the husband and wife have large pupils.

If the corners of large eyes have a pronounced rounded shape the reading is especially positive, being characteristic of people who are humble, sincere, dependable, and loyal to family and friends.

Small Pupils

In face-reading theory, people with unusually small and dark eye pupils tend to be bad characters who instinctively try to destroy anyone who crosses them.

Men with this facial feature may put on a pleasant front but they cannot be taken for granted or trusted. Not surprisingly, they are thin-skinned and have to be handled with special care to avoid rubbing them the wrong way.

Women with small, dark eye pupils tend to be dissatisfied with any kind of settled life, from their work to their relationships with men. In general, tiny black pupils, in both men and women, are said to indicate extraordinary egotism and primitive power that is destructive rather than constructive.

Murderer's Eyes

Most people can recall seeing photographs of revolutionaries, religious fanatics, and killers who were especially violent, and noting something unusual about their eyes. The eye trait that many such people share consists of the pupils of the eyes being "set" above the centerline of the eyes so that a conspicuous portion of the pupils are obscured by the upper eyelids and an unusual amount of "white" shows below the pupils.

In nin so mi, this kind of eye is known as "the murderer's eye," and although people with such eyes do not always become killers, it is a warning that they can be very dangerous. Generally, people with this kind of eyes are cruel, aggressive, and have an overwhelming passion to win in whatever they set out to do, regardless of what it takes.

They tend to be unfriendly and have no scruples about using and betraying others. They may be likely to kill while in a fit of passion, or when committing a crime.

Young men with these eyes tend to be flamboyant in their love affairs. If their interests become political they are the type to use violence to achieve their ends.

Women seldom have "murderer's eyes."

Corners of the Eyes Curve Up

This feature has two different interpretations: one that applies mostly to women and one that applies mostly to men. Where women are concerned, this characteristic is generally taken as a sign of a jealous nature and the inability to express feelings clearly. This results in such women having fewer associations with men and a tendency to delay marriage, making it necessary for them to continue working after marriage. The other reading, which may appear to be contradictory, holds that such women tend to be honest and sincere.

For men, having upturned eye corners is a sign of loyalty, strong resistance to temptation, devotion to work, and pleasant relations with women. Women unconsciously react in a friendly, favorable way to men whose eyes curve upward.

Corners of the Eyes Curve Down

There are also two different readings for this facial trait. In the first reading, found most often in children, the downward slant of the eyes gives an attractive, friendly look. This is a good sign because people react favorably toward them. In the second reading, seen most often in adults, the downward slant of the eyes is generally combined with eyes that are "triangular" in shape. This has negative associations, as this feature is linked to a greedy, unscrupulous nature.

Eyes with Sharp Corners

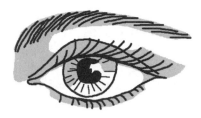

This is a common but unfavorable facial feature. Face-reading lore says it is an indication that the individual concerned is selfish, opportunistic, and uncaring. Such people, they add, tend to engage in get-rich-quick schemes and often make money, but their personality makes it difficult for them to make large amounts of money and keep it. They are also destined to have few friends. Their vision and adaptability tend to be wasted by their attempts to be especially clever.

Eyes with Rounded Corners

This is a very good sign. It is characteristic of a person who is sincere, kind, dependable, humble, and loyal to friends and family. It is also one of the easier eye traits to read because it is very conspicuous. Both men and women are unconsciously attracted to members of both sexes who have this eye feature.

The Sex Sign

This facial trait, which involves the flesh surrounding the inner corner of the eyes, is rather difficult to read, but it is one of the more popular sex-oriented readings in face-reading lore. If these tiny areas are clear, fresh, and bright-looking it means the individual is sexually adequate.

In young people these areas are naturally fair and have a bright luster. They darken gradually as one grows older.

Eyelids That Sag at Inner Corners

This eye feature is characteristic of people who are resourceful and calculating, and is often an indication that they are cold-hearted. Such people are said to do well in business and to be particularly adept at dealing with women. Because of their calculating ways, however, they frequently get into serious trouble with both male and female friends and associates.

Upper Eyelids Raised in the Middle

When the upper eyelids are "raised" or "high" in the middle, it tends to give the eyes a round shape, and is indicative of a person who is artistically inclined, has a flair for music and painting, is sincere and honest, and cares little for money. People with this type of "round eye" are happiest when engaged in some pursuit that allows them to use their artistic talents. They tend to be friendly and enthusiastic about their interests.

Eyelids That Droop in the Middle

Not surprisingly, upper eyelids that "droop" in the middle, giving the individual an odd kind of look, have mixed interpretations that are generally negative. Men with this feature, especially if there are conspicuous horizontal wrinkles on the upper eyelids, are inclined to be cool, shrewd, objective, and overly interested in worldly success.

Women with this feature are often good at business and succeed on their own. If they marry businessmen, they contribute significantly to their success.

The Romance Sign

This feature involves the upper eyelids at the outer corners of the eyes. If the eyelids are "raised" or "high" at these points it is a sign that the person is full of vitality, has a strong personality, and is exceptionally romantic.

Men with this feature have a better than average chance of being successful, whether their goals are success in business or with women, not only because of their innate character but also because the sign sends a positive message.

Where women are concerned this feature can be a mixed bag. They also tend to have a selfish, unyielding nature and to use their sex appeal to manipulate men. If such women are intelligent and clever they can have things pretty much as they want them, making out well in either the business or entertainment fields.

If they are not smart and clever, nin so mi experts say, they more often than not end up being manipulated by men. Women in this category may not be much better off than those with upper eyelids that droop at the outer corners.

The Weak-Will Sign

Upper eyelids that droop at the outer corners are said to be a sign of a wishy-washy person with little willpower who is not very discriminating and is easily influenced by others. Such people naturally tend to be passive, and to be irresponsible. If they come from a good family that gives them guidance and helps them financially, they may do all right. If they are left on their own, or fall in with disreputable people, they will get into trouble. Women with this character and personality are especially vulnerable to mistreatment by more aggressive men

The Unhappy Woman Sign

For cultural reasons, this sign, which also involves the lower eyelids, has traditionally been applied only to women. When the lower eyelids are thin, of poor color, and sag, especially near the inner corners of the eyes, it is an indication of the absence of a youthful spirit, affection, and love.

Women who have this feature tend to be cold, mean, and unattractive. They generally do not enjoy life, and in fact, make life unpleasant for those around them.

After marriage, such women are usually unable to maintain a friendly, affectionate relationship with their husbands, and are prone to take their frustrations out on their children.

As a result, the family atmosphere in such households is typically strained and cold. In these families, the children are likely to leave home even though they are still too young and inexperienced to take care of themselves.

The Good Person Sign

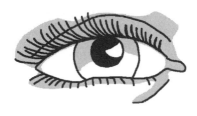

As usual in face reading, there is a Jekyll and Hyde counterpart to thin, sagging lower eyelids. Lower eyelids that are not thin but bulge upward at the center, rather than sag, have a positive connotation. According to the rules of face reading, this is characteristic of people who have pleasant dispositions and are friendly, diplomatic, and gentle.

Men with this feature also tend to be attractive to women. This same feature often appears in women and has similarly positive readings. They typically have happy marriages, get pregnant easily, and have an easy time in labor.

The After-Forty Sign

When the outer portion of the lower eyelid is noticeably raised, the skin around the eyes is usually smooth and fair. This condition is an indication that the person is healthy and youthful. As most people grow older, the skin in this area fades and becomes wrinkled. In some cases, however, this area remains fresh-colored and unwrinkled, and is a sign that these fortunate individuals have retained their youthful vigor.

The Exhaustion Sign

If the outer area of the lower eyelid is concave—that is, curves downward—it may be good or bad, depending on the condition of the skin in the area. If the skin is rough and dark it is a sign that the person is exhausted. This exhaustion may be the result of overeating or drinking. When this condition in a man continues for some time, he becomes less attractive to women. Women with this eyelid condition tend to be discontented.

When the flesh around this type of lower eyelid is fresh and clear, however, the sign is a good one. It is an indication that such people are intelligent, have good manners, and are liked by everyone. Such people do well when their work involves contact with others, and generally will not keep a job long if it requires them to work alone.

Between the Eyes and Eyebrows

As a rule, the wider the space between a person's eyes and eyebrows, and the cleaner and more attractively fleshed the area, the better one's future will be. Nin so mi notes that children born with this feature are given many more chances in life than those born without it. Those with the feature ordinarily develop into gentle, friendly people who tend to be very popular and often become entertainers or politicians.

If the area between the eyes and eyebrows is narrow, however, it is an indication that the individual concerned cannot expect very much help from others and will have to work harder for anything he or she gets.

The less flesh in this area the more likely the person will be practical, cautious, and scrupulous in his or her views. Whatever success these people achieve usually comes late in life.

On a man, if this area is narrow but fleshy, it is regarded as a sign that his youth was spent in poverty, but he is likely to a hard worker, have a strong will, and therefore be more likely to achieve success than a man without the ample flesh.

Women with narrow, fleshless spaces between their eyes and eyebrows are generally not very discriminating, particularly in their preferences in men. Such women tend to pick their mates on the basis of personality, without regard for their background, economic situation, or future potential.

Witch Eyes

Women who have a thick bulge of flesh at the corners of their upper eyelids that cause their eyebrows to protrude and assume a bent-twig shape tend to be sharp-minded and exceptionally sensuous in their manner and appearance. Women in this category also tend to be exceptionally proud, and their pride prevents them from being susceptible to the advances of just any man.

Such women will not be homebody housewives. Housework bores them, and unless they can get into some business that deals with people, they will be dissatisfied and difficult to get along with. Witch-eyed women are especially successful in the entertainment industry. Many actresses have this facial feature. The witch's eye seldom occurs in men.

Satyr Eyes

Young men whose eyes and eyebrows are spaced wide apart, with the area between them presenting a hollow appearance, which results in the whites of the eyes being particularly noticeable, are said to be cold and crafty, specializing in taking advantage of the weaknesses of others. They are said to be especially skillful in bilking women out of their possessions.

Men with this feature are generally the most active and most dangerous when they are in their forties and early fifties and prey primarily on middle-aged and older women.

The Passionate Sign

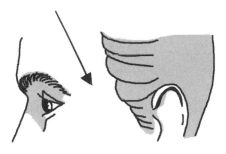

One of the most important and most expressive of the facial features is said by nin so mi experts to be a small spot near the temples, parallel to the corners of the eyes. The key to reading this sign is its condition. If the flesh is rich and vivid in color, it is said to indicate that the person is exceptionally passionate. Both men and women with this sign are said to need the company of the opposite sex to remain content and happy.

If this area is dark and has a hollow appearance, it is a sign of loss of vigor, and indicates that the person is likely to be suffering from bad physical and mental health.

As a person grows older, it is natural for this spot to darken and become wrinkled. If this happens to a woman before her menopause, it is regarded as a sign that she is unhappy with her husband, is likely to divorce him, or he is likely to die early. Women with a negative sign are advised to work outside the home and not remain dependent upon their husbands.

Blue veins appearing in this spot are said to be a sign of serious trouble with one's wife or husband. If this area then becomes dark, it means the problem is reaching the explosion point and separation or divorce is the most likely result.

Fishtail Eyes

The fishtail eye, so called because wrinkles at the outer corners of the eyes resemble the lines in a fish's tail fin, is regarded as a bad omen for husband-and-wife relations. It is said that men and women who fall into this category often do not marry, and that those who do invariably have difficulties that frequently lead to divorce.

Fickle Eyes

People with heavily wrinkled upper eyelids tend to be youthful in their behavior regardless of their age, have likable personalities, and be especially attractive to the opposite sex. Women in this category tend to be exceptionally responsive to the approaches of men, but smart enough to control their relationships.

Men with this type of eyelid are said to be unable to content themselves with one partner, and therefore apt to be fickle.

5

What the Nose Shows

Face readers throughout the world agree that the size and shape of a person's nose is intimately related to social status and to his or her ability to prosper financially.

Short, Flat Noses

A short, flat nose gives off all kinds of messages that are generally unfavorable, and such noses have a decidedly negative impact on how other people perceive their owners. Because people with short, flat noses almost always have other handicaps as well, both physical and mental, the odds are against them accomplishing anything outstanding. People in this category are usually slow thinkers and slow movers, but they may be doggedly loyal to anyone who treats them fairly and kindly, and therefore often make good employees and good friends.

The Short Nose Syndrome

The ideal length of a person's nose is said to be one-third the length of his or her face. Anything less is classified as short; anything over is regarded as long.

There are two distinct categories of men with short noses: those who are of average or above average intelligence and those who are below the average. Intelligent men with short noses are inclined to be flexible, likable, openhearted, not too concerned about the deeper implications of work or life, and prone to make quick decisions.

Such men tend to be popular with everyone and do their work well, but they have a tendency to spend money too freely, which limits the amount of success they are likely to achieve.

Men with short noses who are below average intelligence tend to be irresponsible, dull, and impractical, unable to resist their impulses, and make many mistakes.

Women with short noses are less likely to be dumb, but they have a fickle streak that often results in bumpy relations with boyfriends and husbands, particularly the latter. While short-nosed women do not make ideal wives, they tend to do well in outside careers, especially in entertainment, where their fickle nature is not a handicap.

The Long Nose

The longer people's noses are the less flexible they tend to be, and the more likely they are to take things too seriously. But people with long noses generally have refined tastes and a strong sense of responsibility, and are scrupulous about their work. Long-nosed people are usually not concerned enough about money to make outstanding businesspersons, but they make valuable employees. They also generally do exceptionally well in education and religion.

People with excessively long noses, however, have a problem. They are generally unable to keep in close touch with reality and have difficulty in establishing and maintaining close relationships and in feeling and expressing love. The more extreme the long-nose syndrome, the more pronounced its negative implications.

As is the case with many other physical challenges, some people with exceptionally long noses are able to suppress their natural inclinations to some degree and to overcome the negative reactions people have to their noses by making fun of them or using them to make a point.

Long, Large, High Noses

People who have long, large, high noses are notorious for being stubborn and insisting upon having their own way. If they are intelligent, and most are, they are likely to end up getting their own way through intimidation.

Since too much of anything is bad, noses that are so prominent that they overshadow the rest of the face and figure can be a serious handicap if the person doesn't have some other attribute or skill that mitigates or cancels the negative influence.

And, of course, there are well-known examples of men and women who built careers, or greatly enhanced their careers, on their prominent noses. It is an interesting aspect of nature that people with especially large noses generally develop talents that help them compensate for what otherwise would be a major handicap.

Crooked Noses

Human beings automatically reject disharmony and disorder because such things represent flaws and events that cannot be controlled and are therefore frightening. And there are few facial features that are more disharmonious than crooked noses, whether natural or man-made, and while they do not necessarily frighten anyone (except perhaps infants and toddlers), they nevertheless dramatically affect the reaction of people.

No matter how good their character or how talented and ambitious they may be, people with crooked noses face major obstacles that make it much more difficult, and sometimes impossible, for them to have happy, successful lives.

A crooked nose is especially detrimental to the success of women because they are more often judged on their appearance, particularly when they are young. When women with noticeably crooked noses do marry, the chances of them having a happy marriage are reduced.

For both men and women with crooked noses, the degree of negative influence is determined by how crooked and how conspicuous the nose may be. Obviously, the more crooked and the more conspicuous, the greater the negative influence.

About the only time a crooked nose can be an asset is when it is the result of an accident that is so unusual it makes the person famous, or the person was famous to begin with, and their friends and public "overlook" the nose.

Whether a person can overcome another's reaction to the crooked nose will be determined by his or her intelligence and wit, and of course, this will work only when the person is directly interacting with friends and acquaintances, not with strangers.

Discolored Noses

Having a nose that is any color other than natural is a major handicap because people instinctively hold back from those who look different.

Dark "sooty" noses are indicative of bad health, as well as financial difficulties. People with red noses generally have bad luck in their careers and with money. If they do somehow manage to become wealthy, they generally do not live long enough to enjoy their wealth.

If the pores of one's nose become clogged and the skin turns scaly, it is a very conspicuous sign of bad health and impending bad luck. The clearer and fresher-looking the flesh on the nose, the more likely the individual will be treated well by others, get help when it is needed, and succeed in both personal and work relationships.

Pretty Noses

Some people have noses that are pretty. They are beautifully shaped and have clear, healthy skin that signals not only good health but tells a lot about the personalities of the people. Both men and women with pretty noses tend to be fond of music and the fine arts, and to dislike anything that is harsh or rough. Their taste in food is also likely to be refined.

Men with shapely noses tend to be fancy dressers and take it for granted that women find them attractive—which is often true because of their other qualities. Women with finely shaped noses, however, tend to be vain and to judge everything and everybody by appearance, especially if their other facial features are plain or ugly.

Childish Noses

A few people—most often women—have very small "baby noses" that never grew up—or out. Regardless of how intelligent such people may be, a tiny nose is generally regarded as a sign of a low I.Q., lack of imagination, and overall immaturity. They are usually followers rather than leaders, and on the bottom rung of whatever group they are a part.

Women with baby noses are especially vulnerable to aggressive men, and nin so mi records show that they are also especially susceptible to becoming pregnant. Such women tend to be poor home managers. Tiny-nosed women are advised to marry men who work with their hands and have unsophisticated tastes.

Humpbacked Noses

Both men and women can have humpbacked noses, but this feature is far more common in men. Men with humpbacked noses who are physically strong are inclined to be strong-willed, adventurous, impatient, and uncompromising. They make good military officers and explorers but bad salesmen.

Women with humpbacked noses demonstrate some of the same character traits that distinguish humpbacked-nose men, which results in them regularly clashing with men, since both want their own way and do not like to give in or lose.

Men as well as women who have humpbacked noses tend to be less than brilliant.

Women with noses that are both humpbacked and small tend to be very scrupulous and efficient in their work, at home as well as outside, but care little for relationships with men.

Money-Bag Noses

Much of face-reading theory is borne out by folk wisdom that dates from the earliest civilizations. One such instance is the so-called bag-nose facial feature. A "bag" nose by definition is a nose that, from a profile view, looks something like a bag because it "droops over." And not surprisingly, it gets its name from the fact that people with this kind of nose tend to have an overriding interest in possessions, particularly money, which one might carry around in a bag.

In addition to indicating people who tend to measure everything in terms of money, bag-nosed people are inclined to be clever, unscrupulous, heartless, and take advantage of every possible opportunity to make a profit.

The bag nose is almost never seen in people with little interest in accumulating possessions.

Male Humanist Noses

Men who have strong-looking, solid noses with a slight convex or upward curve in the center are believed to be a rare but welcome blessing to mankind, because they tend to be honest, trustworthy, and have genuine love and respect for their fellowmen.

Men who have this so-called humanist nose more likely than not live in harmony with everyone, are constructive rather than destructive, and do not have any serious downs in their lives.

It is usually easy to spot men with this kind of nose. They are generally taller than the average male, with solid builds to go with their noses. They are also conspicuous, because they tend to be leaders in whatever enterprise they engage in. Women, therefore, find such men unusually attractive, resulting in them meeting and marrying women of exceptional beauty and talents.

The Feminine Nose

Of all the different types of noses, the one most common among women is finely shaped, not too big or too small for the face it adorns, and has a ridge that is slightly concave, rising in a very harmonious slant all the way to the tip of the nose.

Women with this typically female nose generally demonstrate all the more pleasing characteristics associated with the ideal female image. They have a strong interest in aesthetics and like neatness, order, and pretty things. They want children and make good mothers.

Women with finely shaped noses and concave bridges also enjoy entertainment, and have successful careers in that field. However, usually only those who work very hard to develop some special talent are able to continue this success throughout their lives.

On the down side, women with this facial feature are generally not strong physically or emotionally, are susceptible to being used and abused by stronger personalities, and need the care and support of family and friends. And just as often, they are not wise enough to seek this kind of supporting relationship.

The Successful Person's Nose

It is amazing how much something as mundane as a nose or its nostrils have to do with a person's success or failure, and the successful person's nose is a good example. Nostrils may seem undistinguishable, but they do in fact differ. Some have really tiny holes, while others are large and wide to the point of being unsightly.

Over many centuries, nin so mi scholars scrutinized people who went from "rags to riches." One of the things these scholars discovered was that a disproportionate number of these success-ful men had rather small noses with nostrils that "flared out."

Nin so mi experts recorded that men with flared nostrils had unusually dynamic personalities, did not care much for appearances, minor details, or complicated paperwork, but were exceptionally good at business, which more often than not led to significant success.

The Creative Person's Nose

The idea of predicting future criminal behavior from the shape of a person's head has been discounted, but what about being able to pick out people who may become the great inventors and creators of the future?

Nin so mi masters say it is possible—and all you have to do is check out the noses of people from their late teens on up. Face-reading masters say that a well-shaped nose that droops slightly downward at the end, but does not "hook" or become a "bag," is a sign of extraordinary creativity.

You might say that these people follow their noses, looking at things with far more curiosity and care than the average person. This leads them to delve into how things work, why they work that way, and then try to come up with a better way.

This creativity sign applies to both men and women.

The Analyst's Nose

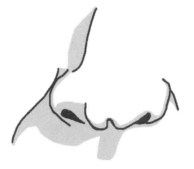

This nose, formed by a cleft at the tip, is rare but ranks high on the list of those that are the most conspicuous, and you are unlikely to forget anyone you meet who has one.

The cleft in this nose is pronounced enough that the two sides form easily discernible divisions or lobes. The deeper the nose cleft and the more conspicuous the lobes, the stronger their implications.

People with this kind of nose are skeptics who analyze everything and will not stop until they see or hear proof of every proposition. And they are not satisfied unless the proof is totally convincing.

Because of their skepticism and analytical nature, people in this category tend to be argumentative and have difficulty getting along with people. Analytical-nosed people are generally much better off in work that is narrow in scope and allows them to work alone. Scholars often have this type of nose.

6

Messages from the Mouth

The Large Mouth

The mouth is one of the strongest indicators of attitudes about love and food, and overall personality—and it speaks long before it is ever opened. People with large mouths and thick lips almost always have unrestrained appetites—for everything.

As a rule, men and women with large mouths live expansively. Their energy, ambitions, and outgoing manner, if coupled with intelligence, provide them with extraordinary opportunities for success.

But there are several categories of large mouths and it is necessary to distinguish between them to get an accurate reading. Some large mouths are thick and others are thin. Some are loose and some are tight. People with large, tight mouths tend to be unusually able, to be daring and capable of great things in business or politics. Many of the great leaders of the past had large, tight mouths.

People with large, thin mouths may have equally strong appetites, but their behavior is more calculated and controlled, so they do not stir up as many waves.

A large loose mouth is definitely an undesirable sign. It is automatically associated with unrestrained behavior that ranges from unsightly and annoying to seriously disturbing and sometimes dangerous. The looser the large mouth the more likely the individual is to be severely challenged by life.

Women who have large, shapely, firm mouths tend to be very active, friendly, and popular. They often become so involved in outside interests that their home lives and marriages suffer. The chances of their first marriage falling apart are quite high. Most women who become noted for their civic activities have large, firm mouths.

A large, firm female mouth can be intimidating to men who are not fully confident of their masculinity. Most men admire such women but the majority shy away from them.

The Small Mouth

Conspicuously small mouths are associated with weakness, timidity, dependence, emotionalism, and other undesirable characteristics. Most of the genes for small mouths are surely inherited, but nin so mi says that excessive pampering during infancy and childhood is both a cause and a result of small mouths.

One of the reasons for such excess pampering is that children born with exceptionally small mouths appear more infantile than children with normal-sized mouths, and elicit more pampering behavior from their parents and other adults.

This pampering, according to face-reading logic, interferes with the normal development of such children, so that they end up being doubly handicapped.

Men with small mouths have fewer chances for success in life because people do not react to them as positively as they react to others, and these men also tend to lack courage, resourcefulness, and other leadership qualities. Small-mouthed men are prone to act on their personal feelings rather than on an objective appraisal of situations.

Face-reading theory holds that men with small mouths who do succeed in business because of other traits are likely to fail after they pass middle age. It is also said that men with small mouths are best suited for jobs that call for neatness and precision and little interaction with others.

Both men and women with small mouths and thin lips tend to be self-centered and callous toward others, with women more likely being the exceptions.

Whether the lips are loose or tight has a great deal to do with the reading of small mouths. Small mouths with tight lips are indicative of ambition and a fighting spirit. Loose lips and a small mouth are a sign of sensuality and an easygoing relaxed attitude. Most men are attracted to women with medium-sized to small mouths because they present a weaker image than women with big mouths, and men subconsciously assume they have an advantage over them.

The negative readings and consequences of an unusually small mouth can be partially overcome by extraordinary intelligence, cleverness, a sharp wit, and special physical skills—but on the average, people with small mouths do not have these attributes.

All other things being equal, a small, finely shaped mouth is associated with a rather cold nature—and someone who gets no special pleasure out of food. There are, however, many examples of people with small mouths who have succeeded admirably in many endeavors, from business and politics to singing.

The Protruding Mouth

Seen in profile, some people's mouths protrude beyond the line of their nose and chin. In face-reading theory, this is a sign of low intelligence and stubbornness, and usually indicates that the individual is strongly opinionated.

The mouths of people who have a reputation for being big talkers and talking too much often fit into this category. And not surprisingly, they often become salesmen, politicians, or entertainers.

Women with protruding mouths are usually not popular with men for obvious reasons, but women are often attracted to men with protruding mouths because their outgoing talkativeness is subconsciously interpreted as a business asset that will contribute to their financial security.

Convex Mouths with Thick Lips

You've seen this kind of mouth before. It is often used in cartoons to caricature people in a negative light. People with thick lips and a mouth that curves downward at the corners tend to be argumentative, always complaining, and unwilling to take the advice of others.

Women with this mouth are prone to be cool- to cold-natured, wanton, strong-willed, easily spoiled by luxury, and to make decisions quickly based on their emotions only.

This mouth gives off unfriendly associations and is especially disadvantageous for women, because so much of their success in life depends on making people feel good. Men with convex mouths and thick lips are generally able to get by because they are not expected to present a "Mr. Feel Good" image all the time.

Concave Mouths with Thick Lips

This is one of the most desirable types of mouths because it indicates a kind heart and warm personality. In addition, people with this kind of mouth are usually adaptable and efficient, and therefore make a good impression on others.

However, people with this type of mouth are not leaders. They prefer to let others make the decisions.

Straight Mouths with Thick Lips

Many people have mouths that have almost perfectly straight mouth lines and relatively thick lips. This is not a bad mouth to have, but it has its limitations. People in this category are usually reserved in both their attitudes and behavior, and emphasize the practical realities of life.

Because of the practical nature of people in this group, they generally do not have big dreams and are not motivated by uplifting ideals.

Thick and Thin Upper Lips

The upper lip is said to reflect the depth of one's affection for others. The thicker the upper lip, the deeper the person's outgoing affections. People with unusually thick upper lips are also said to be unusually kind and well mannered, and especially fond of the opposite sex.

Men with thick upper lips typically spare no effort or expense to have relationships with many women. Women in the same lip group are also especially passionate, and unless they are smart enough to resist their impulses they may ruin their lives.

When both the upper and lower lips are thick, it is a conspicuous sign of strong sensuality and boldness. People who are in this category are seldom satisfied with one person, and are advised by nin so mi practitioners to work in businesses where they can meet members of the opposite sex.

Thin Upper Lip

Thin lips send out messages that are exactly the opposite of thick lips—a cool nature, little sensuality, and an attitude that links passion with sin.

Women with thin upper lips are often fleshy, and are often taken advantage of by aggressive men

Men who marry women with thin upper lips do not necessarily have unhappy lives, because the wives are usually not jealous and are affectionate enough to maintain a fairly harmonious relationship with their husbands.

Lips of Conceit

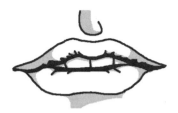

Most people are familiar with these lips because they are often seen in entertainers and politicians. The so-called lips of conceit occur when the upper lip is raised in the center to the extent that the upper teeth are partially visible.

In face-reading theory, this lip reveals strong feelings of superiority, ability, appearance, and, often, physical strength as well. While people with this facial feature often appear warm and friendly, it is more a public show. These people are also susceptible to flattery.

The Drooping Mouth

Everyone has seen a clown with a sad face. This sad look is achieved by making the mouth droop or curve down on each side. A naturally drooping mouth is a sign of significant problems in a person's psychological makeup.

In addition to attracting negative responses from other people, drooping mouths indicate a cold, unfriendly nature that makes it difficult for such individuals to have warm, friendly relations with other people.

People with this mouth may succeed in business if the job doesn't depend too much on personal relationships. In addition to turning people off, a drooping mouth is also an indication that the individual concerned has some kind of health problem.

On the plus side, if a woman has a droopy mouth that is also rather large, she is likely to be an especially hard worker.

Lips of Enthusiasm

When the center of the upper lip forms a downward *V* shape, it indicates a person who is full of enthusiasm and very devoted. Whatever people in this category do, they do it with great energy, concentration, patience, and diligence. This type of upper lip is often found among people of higher intelligence.

When this area of the upper lip is "raised" or curves upward, however, it is a sign of impatience, moodiness, and the inability to stick to one thing. It is said that women who have this feature are ideally suited for the entertainment industry.

Protruding Lower Lip

Women whose lower lip and lower teeth protrude (as a result of a protruding chin) are regarded as being unable to get along well with men. Such women are said to be incapable of showing very much affection for the opposite sex.

Women with this type of lip are advised to work and not be completely dependent upon their husbands, otherwise they may face an unhappy home life.

Lower Lip Recessed

As might be expected, a small, recessed lower lip is regarded as a sign of weak character and passivity. People with this kind of mouth are generally undependable and unable to make their own way. Men with thin, recessed lower lips are advised to work for large, bureaucratic organizations, like the government. Women in this category are no match for sharp, aggressive men, and are advised to marry stable, factory-worker types who appreciate their passivity.

Lips That Are Uneven

People with uneven or off-center lips tend to be high-strung, hot-tempered, and opinionated. They are seldom able to associate with anyone for any length of time without getting into an argument. Such people are advised to seek jobs in which they can work alone. There is a tendency for people in this category to use humor to communicate effectively with others, and some have gone on to become famous as comics.

Lip Wrinkles and Lip Color

Deep wrinkles on the lower lip are a sign of addiction to eating and drinking. People with this trait are generally free-spenders, affectionate, and popular. They usually get along well with the opposite sex.

The color of the lips also plays an important role in face reading. Purplish lips are said to be a sign of a serious disease. Unusually bright red lips are associated with respiratory illnesses. Generally, pale lips indicate poor health, and pink lips are a sign of good health and vitality.

Bright red lips can also be a sign of sexual interest, which explains why lipstick is so popular. The brighter the red, the stronger the invitation.

The "Deep" Upper Lip

The "grooved" space between the bottom of the nose and the top of the upper lip is one of the most important of all facial features because of the strength of the message it sends. In nin so mi, this space is called the *jinchu* (*jeen-chuu*), which means something like "at the front."

A long jinchu is definitely preferable to a short one. A long space between the nose and mouth is an indication of "high birth," a powerful life force, and a strong drive.

Exceptionally beautiful women and handsome men invariably have well-defined, longish jinchu. It is also an attribute that is conspicuous in unusually successful men and women whether or not they have physically attractive faces. Many famous persons—entertainers, businesspeople, and politicians—have conspicuously long jinchu.

Not everyone who has a long jinchu lives to an advanced age, but most men who live to eighty and beyond almost always do.

A short jinchu, especially if it is conspicuously short, is associated with "low birth" and low intelligence. People with short jinchu are usually at the bottom of the cultural and social ladders, and often have large families that contribute to keeping them there. According to face-reading lore, women who have vertical wrinkles on their jinchu are having marital problems.

The Upper Lip Groove

The "groove" on this part of the upper lip is also important in face reading. For the best reading, it should be pronounced, with double-track lines that are straight and well defined. And generally speaking, the wider the upper lip groove the better.

A wide groove coupled with a long space indicates physical and mental vigor. A narrow groove, on the other hand, indicates weakness and timidity.

Any blemish on this part of the face, whether a mole, scar, or wrinkles, has a negative influence on the way people perceive and react to the individual concerned.

The Smiling Mouth

In contrast to the line of the mouth curving downward at the corners, those that curve up, which is characteristic of a smiling face, give off positive readings. When people smile it tends to pull the corners of their mouths upward. Some people's mouths naturally curve upward and they appear to be smiling or at least to have a pleasant look on their faces all the time.

This is a very positive mouth to have. Women with this mouth tend to be gentle, friendly, good-natured, and to enjoy life whether or not they are attractive or have any special talent. One of the key reasons for this is that people respond to them in a positive way.

The same readings generally apply for men as well, but if the sides of the mouth are "loose" the men concerned tend to be ineffective in their efforts and are not as likely to achieve any special success in life.

The Civilized Mouth

The mouth that is well balanced, finely formed, and rather delicately made is indicative of a high order of civilization. People with this type of mouth are most likely to have been obedient and well behaved when young, and to have pleasant personalities and be unselfish and diplomatic once they reach adulthood.

Interestingly, people with this type of mouth are seldom successful financially or politically, but they tend to live happy, useful lives, enjoying harmonious relations with their spouses, children, and the world at large.

The Superman Sign

Super-successful men almost always have a number of facial features in common, including formidable noses; large, "tight" mouths; and vertically long, thick upper lips (where the mustache grows). These are invariably signs of energy, ambition—often combined with high intelligence—and a special gift for taking advantage of the power and influence of others. Many men at the head of giant corporations and in national politics have this type of mouth.

The Two Front Teeth

Front teeth have a lot to do with the way people feel about themselves, with their attitudes and behavior, and with how other people react to them. The size and positioning of the two front teeth are the key factors. If they are conspicuously larger than the other teeth, it means the individual has a friendly nature, is sociable, and loves a good time.

Both men and women with conspicuously large front teeth tend to be showy in their behavior, and to be much more passionate than people with small front teeth. However, if the front teeth of men or women protrude, their influence changes. In this case men are less likely to be taken as seriously by other men, and women are seen as less desirable mates because they are inclined to be pushy and talkative. Men generally like and enjoy such women, as long as they are not married to them.

Women with small chins as well as two large front teeth are doubly handicapped because this combination means they are not only talkative but meddlesome as well.

Teeth That Stick Out

People with projecting teeth almost always have very distinctive personalities that set them apart. Nine times out of ten they are cheerful, showy, aggressive, talkative, and unable to keep secrets.

People whose teeth project outward only moderately tend to be oblivious to criticism, and to have unshakable convictions that often lead them to success. If the projection of the teeth is extreme, however, it becomes a serious handicap and usually prevents the individual from achieving anything outstanding.

Where women are concerned, projecting teeth mean serious marital problems. Women with this type of teeth, being aggressive and big talkers, have the best chances of success in civic or political activities.

Reading the Cheek Wrinkles

The two cheek wrinkles that radiate out from the nose and curve downward are said to be intimately related to one's social and economic status. As people become firmly established in business and society, the depth of these twin wrinkles gradually increases. Responsibility and hard work also deepen these lines—even in those who are very young.

Lack of these two lines in an adult, or very shallow cheek wrinkles, is regarded as a sign that the individual is either inherently incapable or a late-bloomer.

People who have inherited wealth and high social position for generations generally have finely shaped and well-developed cheek wrinkles.

The ideal cheek wrinkles are crescent-shaped. In the event these important lines are straight or ragged rather than gently curved, they are said to be a handicap.

Where women are concerned, if a second set of wrinkles should appear in this area it is said to be a sign that their marriage will end in divorce. Such women, however, are said to do especially well in business and to be popular with their superiors.

Cheek wrinkles that run into the mouth are regarded as a bad sign, and are believed to be an indication that people with this feature cannot support themselves or take care of their affairs. In the most severe cases, this feature is thought to be a signal that the individual is in bad health and may not have long to live.

On occasion, wrinkles from beneath a person's lower lip will connect with the cheek wrinkles. This generally occurs only in men, and is regarded as a sign that they will have serious marital problems.

A total lack of cheek wrinkles in mature adults indicates irresponsibility and instability. People in this group are notorious for habitually changing jobs and occupations.

7

Check Those Ears!

Large Ears

The size, position, and quality of the ears are very important in determining the character, personality, talents, and longevity of people. Large ears are indicative of courage and initiative, and are associated with long life. If the earlobes are also large and firm, then the large ears mean significant success, particularly in business and politics. Most people who live to be very old and attain great success have ears that are conspicuously large. Not surprisingly, thick, hard earlobes are also a sign of good health.

People with large ears are generally not intellectuals, but they are often intelligent, street-smart, hardworking, patient, and persistent—which accounts for the success they achieve. Not all large ears are good. If ears are too large for the head, or if they are crooked or stick out, the readings and their influence become negative.

What Small Ears Say

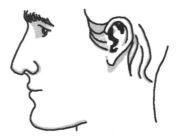

Small ears—those that are noticeably below the average size but not extremely small—are not all bad. Although they indicate that the individual has a tendency to be flighty and to have a bad memory, small ears are also a sign that the individual is artistic and creative. However, artistic and creative talent does not appear until middle age, and in their younger years such people may be regarded as losers.

Ears Large in the Upper Portion

Most people have ears that are fairly well balanced between the upper and lower portions. But in some there are significant differences. Some people have ears that are conspicuously large in the upper area and proportionately small in the lobe area. Others are just the reverse: large, long lobes and small upper areas.

People with ears that are especially large in the upper part are generally very intelligent and have extraordinary memories. They are usually vigorous and aggressive, have a strong sense of responsibility, and often accomplish great things. It is almost axiomatic that the more successful a person in non-artistic fields, the more likely it is that he or she will have ears that are conspicuously large.

Ears Large in the Lower Portion

Successful people—in business and sports, especially—often have ears that are proportionately larger at the bottom than at the top, with long, thick earlobes. If other features are favorable, people in this category tend to be fun- and pleasure-loving and are expansive in their pursuit of both.

People with ears that are large in the lobe area and small on top tend to take life much less seriously than those with ears that are larger in the upper portion. They tend to prefer sports and entertainment to other kinds of business.

The Ears of Nobility

Nin so mi experts believe that both the position and quality of the ears are related to one's social background. They say that ears that are located lower on the head than usual are a sure sign of social or class superiority.

If the tops of the ears are below the level of the eyes, they are said to be an unerring sign of nobility. Check your mirror. You may be a long-lost descendant of a king!

8

The Reality of Face Reading

As noted at the beginning of this book, face reading is a natural, normal practice that all of us engage in every time we meet people, regardless of who they are or how often we meet them—including family members with whom we live. We even read our own faces every time we look into a mirror.

It therefore stands to reason that developing skill in face reading beyond what comes naturally to the average person can be a very valuable asset.

However, despite its obvious merits, face reading is not a see-all, know-all science. It is part instinct and part intuition, neither of which can be absolutely quantified. Furthermore, the instinctive and intuitive abilities of individuals vary greatly, depending on their genetic makeup, the environment in which they are raised, and their personal experiences.

And there is more. Nature genetically programs people to have certain predispositions, to react positively to some things and negatively to others. While cultural influences can determine whether men prefer fat or slender women, and whether women prefer men who are gentle and kind or rough and callous, there are many things that are built into human nature.

These genetically programmed dispositions include an innate preference for balanced, harmonious facial features, for big eyes, for well-proportioned lips, and so on. I believe this programming is the basis for the validity of the more obvious face readings.

Then we get into areas that cannot be seen or easily read from one's appearance, areas in which the character, personality, and success or failure of the individual does not seem to be related to the facial features.

There are extremely ugly people—meaning that their facial features are not balanced, not harmonious, not attractive—and yet they achieve extraordinary success in a broad range of fields. There are many entertainers, for example, whose faces would scare babies, and yet they achieve the pinnacle of success.

The reason why such people are able to overcome the handicap of an unbalanced, unattractive face is that they are driven by some deep-seated impulse to work very hard to develop skills or talents that set them apart and allow them to rise above the average.

Another factor is that some people are literally born with built-in talents that have only to be allowed to grow for them to achieve success, and these preprogrammed talents are unrelated to their facial features. Nature is funny that way. Even in social situations involving male-female interactions, people with unattractive faces are often loved and cherished because of other attributes that endear them.

Finally, just being able to read facial features will not give you a complete picture of an individual's character, personality, sexuality, or success.

It is also necessary to consider the power of the individual's drive—the "force" that motivates them. Some people have very powerful drives; others seem to have none at all. Judging people by their appearance alone is less than half of the equation.

Still, it is obvious that people who are good-looking have more opportunities than most, and are more likely to succeed, particularly in business, entertainment, and politics. Of course, some of these people go on to develop their talents, others don't.

In the end, the more balanced and attractive a person's facial features—especially the larger and more attractive their eyes, because eyes are the primary focal point of the face—the more positive people feel toward them and the more they are catered to, generally making life and success easier.

For better or worse, looks count, so the challenge is to look as good as you can—and to make the most of your appearance—no matter what you start out with.

9

Changing Your Fortune

People are limited in what they can do to change their basic body build, but there are several things they can do to change their facial appearance—and thereby change their fortune.

Moles and scars can be made less conspicuous or removed entirely. A man can grow a beard to cover an undersized chin or hide unsightly scars and skin imperfections. Men can also wear their hair long or short, parted or straight.

Women have even more socially approved leeway in what they can do to alter their facial appearance—and their fortune. With the marvel of makeup, hairstyling, and dress, it is often possible for a plain-looking woman to transform herself into a glamorous woman.

And, of course, both men and women with more serious facial faults—crooked or oversized noses, protruding teeth—can have them corrected by simple surgical techniques.

Given that their fortunes are at stake, people should not hesitate to make any improvements in their faces that are reasonable and possible.